in a splash
from my paddle
rainbow

Other Works by Cor van den Heuvel

sun in skull [Haiku], Chant Press, New York City, 1961.

a bag of marbles (3 Jazz Chants), Chant Press, 1962.

the window-washer's pail [Haiku], Chant Press, 1963.

E07 [Haiku Sequence], Chant Press, 1964.

BANG! you're dead [Poem], Chant Press, 1966.

water in a stone depression [Haiku], Chant Press, 1969.

dark [Haiku], Chant Press, 1982.

PUDDLES [Haibun], Chant Press, 1990.

The Geese Have Gone [Haiku], King's Road Press, Pointe Claire, Quebec, 1992.

Play Ball [Baseball Haiku], Red Moon Press, Winchester, Virginia, 1999.

A Boy's Seasons: Haibun Memoirs, Single Island Press, Portsmouth, New Hampshire, 2010.

At the Top of the Ferris Wheel: Selected Haiku of Cor van den Heuvel, Red Moon Press, Winchester, VA, 2017.

As Editor:

The Haiku Anthology, Doubleday Anchor, New York City, 1974; Simon & Schuster, New York City, 1986; W.W. Norton, New York City, 1999.

The Haiku Path, (Co-Editor with various others), The Haiku Society of America, New York City, 1994.

Wedge of Light [Haibun], (Co-Editor with Tom Lynch and Michael Dylan Welch), Press Here, Foster City, California, 1999.

Past Time [Baseball Haiku], (Co-Editor with Jim Kacian), Red Moon Press, Winchester, Virginia, 1999.

Baseball Haiku, (Co-Editor with Nanae Tamura), W.W. Norton, New York City, 2007.

Cor van den Heuvel

Splashes

HOUSE
OF HAIKU

Copyright © 2023 by Cor van den Heuvel

All rights reserved.

First Edition
Printed in the United States of America

ISBN 978-0-9626040-5-8

House of Haiku
Kernersville, NC
houseofhaiku.com

Cover photograph (Shenandoah National Park)
by Katy Cain, National Park Service

Back cover photograph of Cor van den Heuvel
by Donna Beaver

All haiga artwork by Cor van den Heuvel

Book Design by Donna Beaver

To
my niece Sharyn Esposito
and my son Dirk van den Heuvel
for helping me to keep my hands
on the Plow

Contents

PART A: Haibun from Notebooks
Blobs?	2
Wings	4
At The Lake	8
Three Birds	12
Walking the Beach	14
The Wasp	15
Joyful Things	17
Fireflies	18
The Flying Seed	20
The Click Bug, Etc.	23
The Winter Wren	25
The Katydid	28
The Pod	31
The Duel	32
Mergansers, Mergansers	33

Seven Haiga Sketches ... 37

PART B: Haibun for Basho's Frog
Hitch-Hiking	48
The Last Street Light	50
Stepping Up To The Bar	67
Curbstones	83
The Sign	87
The Cricket	90
The Squirrel	94
The Singer	96
Yellow	99
Snowstorm	100
Puddles	101

Credits ... 108

PART A:
Haibun from Notebooks

Blobs?

September 16, 1972

Nice sunny day—cool breeze, occasionally, during quite a warm afternoon—blue skies.

Spent an hour or so at the Metropolitan Museum of Art—went to see some Kensetts, but only one was hanging: "Lake George" with an overcast view of the lake. It didn't get to me, but I stood ecstatic before Gifford's "Kauterskill Falls" for a long time. (It was next to the "Lake George.") And also (not dreamed) but "envisioned" while looking at a wonderful Bierstadt: "In the Rocky Mountains." Not the one with the Indians, but with the two deer (or elk) in the foreground. (Amazing how the vision becomes just blobs! of paint when one gets too close to the canvas. One has to move back and let the paint create its magic. In the same way a few "blobs" of words, if expertly chosen and placed can also work a similar magic if the mind's ear steps back and lets the words work their wonder.)

Church's "Cotopaxi" another miracle! Also enjoyed a couple of Inness's—and a fine painting of a shipwreck by Bradford, which rendered a shaft of light on one part of the water, and in the full sail of a small boat rescuing the men, with such accuracy and love my heart just swept right into it.

Just before the museum closed, I rushed over to the European galleries to get a quick look at two old favorites: Vermeer's young girl with a lute and his young girl with a water pitcher.

As the guard urged us out of the galleries, I winked at old van Rijn hanging in a corner.

>   in a small museum *
>   Blakelock's "Poetry of Moonlight"
>   shimmers in a forest pool

* in Huntington, Long Island

Wings

October 10, 1972—NYC

This is about a 2-day canoe trip in the Adirondacks that I took on October 4th and 5th (Wed. & Thurs.).

It began at the canoe marina at Fish Creek Ponds at 11 AM Wed. after spending the night in a motel on Saranac Lake: —a beautiful, brisk, sunny fall day / blue sky, blue waters / bright—as I paddled into Square Pond I heard a lot of honking to the north. In a few minutes, I made out high in the sky a huge flock of geese (Canadian, I think) flying south in an almost perfect "V" formation—there must have been at least fifty of them. They "talked" to each other all the way, and I could still hear their (now) faint honking after they faded to nothingness in the sky—lost to my vision. A propitious start.

There was a good breeze coming across Square Pond as I headed across it to Fish Creek—but once in the creek everything was calm and peaceful with that divine combination found only in autumn of clean, clear air and warm sunlight. Dragonflies darted about, glittering in the light: purple ones, crimson, checkerboard designs, etc. and I soon came upon a large turtle sunning himself on a log, his head stretched up into the light—either to bask, or to watch me! I eased up close to him with the canoe, and he let me get to within a paddle's length before diving into the water.

A few minutes later—a little further upstream—I discovered a heron, his head sticking up among some reeds. At first I thought it was some driftwood which had gotten lodged in the mud in an upright position, but I soon made out it was a bird. I let the canoe drift in close to him, and got to about two canoe lengths away when the great wings seemed to come out of nowhere on either side of him and lifted him up in the air—and he flapped lazily, majestically downstream.

I then paddled into Copperas Pond. After crossing it, I carried the canoe about ¼ of a mile to Whey Pond along a portage trail ("carry"). I then paddled the length of Whey to a short carry into Rollins Pond. (On Whey some "foresters" were stocking the waters with fish from a small motorboat.)

Rollins Pond is like a large lake and has a few islands on it. After paddling almost to the north end, I decided to set up camp on a beautiful island there. It was now late afternoon, the sun was getting low. After setting up camp and taking a quick dip in the cold waters, I canoed back out to take some pictures in the light of the sunset. I shot a number of the island which was like a large ship of pines and birches—mostly pines. There was one large birch on the north side whose leaves had all turned a beautiful orange. I then paddled around a nearby point to take shots of some smaller islands with the sun dropping behind them.

I slept well that night after sitting up awhile with a small campfire built against a huge rock. I could see the stars through the branches of the pines and toward morning caught sight of Orion under the branches of a nearby tree as he rose up in the east. There were some small animals splashing around in the waters about the island, but I couldn't get a good look at them. I suppose they were either muskrats or otters. There were a lot of mussel shells around the edge of the island.

Next morning there was a nice sunrise with mist rising off the water, so I took a shot of it. After breakfast and cleaning up camp, I took off in the canoe again for the north shore of the pond. A short distance from the island I noticed in the now clear light of the sunrise a number of autumn leaves floating in the waters around me. A glittering light in one of them caught my eye. It was a drop of water in the curl of the leaf reflecting the rising sun. The leaf sailed on carrying its sparkling cargo, its stem upraised like the prow of a ship.

After paddling around the north shore of Rollins Pond, I found the outlet and followed the shallow stream to Floodwood Pond. Just before reaching Floodwood, I saw a large osprey fly out of a tall pine and "shoulder" its way heavily through the branches of another to disappear beyond it.

The contrast in flight between this bird and the heron I'd seen the day before was striking. Here I felt the muscular strength of the bird's body and the shorter wings as it seemed to disdainfully leave my presence. With the heron it was all wings and grace.

I then paddled around Floodwood Pond and stopped around noon at a small beach for a quick dip, in the nude, and some lunch. I'd seen no one at all on Rollins or Floodwood, though in one of the bays of Floodwood (far from my little beach) I did see someone near a cabin.

I took some shots of trees along the shores of Floodwood and, later, on the stream leading to Little Square Pond which I traveled to next in my canoe. I got close to a muskrat frolicking in the stream, but failed to get a picture. I didn't stay long on Little Square, but headed down Fish Creek to get some shots of trees I'd noticed the day before. I got some nice ones, including some of a group of beautiful golden larches (tamaracks).

Got back to the canoe marina just as darkness fell—to end a perfect outing. Drove back to Saranac Lake for a steak supper and then to sleep in a motel. Headed back to NYC the next day, Friday—speeded most of the way hoping to see Leigh that evening, but she wasn't home. I called her the next day and we had a lovely time that night.

> morning moon
> a heron arrives silently
> among the reeds

*

At The Lake

July 24, 1978—Lake Dutchess, NY

Beautiful double-feature sunset this evening. First, the sky was covered with blue and white variations all across the zenith. The broken cloudcover filtered the light into a million soft shades of blues, grays, whites, and touches of pink. The soft blues that came in from the sky itself set me laughing like crazy at one point.

Then things died down. The sky above turned dark blue—no clouds. A massive bank of clouds in the west was a cold blue-black—the sun was gone to a faint, dull, cold yellow glow that showed below the dark cloud bank. It seemed all over.

Slowly the whole bank began to glow with golds, yellows, oranges and to break up into long feathery shapes—a sunset which, as I said under my breath, would have made an artist like Frederic Church green with envy.

This second "feature" was almost as long as the first—about 10 to 15 minutes, before it faded off into twilight and dusk. I hollered over to Bob (who had been watching the show with Pat from their rowboat) "Try setting that to music." (He's a musician.) "It was certainly worth the price of admission," he called back.

During the "first" feature, a small head poked out of the water and seemed to be watching it also. It stayed up one time for at least two minutes, perhaps more. It popped up in three different spots, four or five feet apart. All about twenty feet away from the shore, where it is about eight feet deep. It seemed about the size and shape of a small turtle's head—sort of triangular shaped.

It stuck out about 1½ inches above the surface of the water. Too dark to tell if it was a turtle, frog, fish or what—but it stayed too still to be a fish. Snake?

Just before the sunset, I saw a lot of different birds: a thrush, a red-winged blackbird, a small reddish-orange bird (half the size of a cardinal) (tanager?), and a small woodpecker. Plus a lot of dark birds—catbirds? Etc. Many swept high above the lake during the sunset.

July 25, 1978—Lake Dutchess

a radio announcer
praises last night's
sunset

July 30, 1978—Lake Dutchess

Bright, windy day. Sunny blue sky with white, fleecy clouds. Rowed around south end of the lake—explored the water-lily cove, near Sailboat Rock, and later the Island of the Lake. Saw a large "fly-like" insect standing on top of a closed water-lily bud. It had long legs, so that its body was ½ inch above the bud. It was the exoskeleton of the bug for it was hollow! And all dried out. I don't know what was holding it to the bud in such breezy weather (almost like a fall day)—for I lifted it off easily. I had seen three of these same bug-skeletons standing on the metal posts holding my dock. I'd thought then that they'd been sucked dry by a spider. But a spider could not have killed this one in the middle of the lake.

Also saw four or five turtles sunning themselves on the rocks—but they all slipped into the water before I could get close. Several minutes later, a small head poked up out of the water about six feet away from the rocks, and looked around as if to see if I was still there. It looked like the small head I'd seen stick out of the water during the spectacular sunset last Monday. Was it a turtle that evening?

By a small island further south on the lake, I tied up the boat and took a swim. While inspecting some rocks next to the island, I climbed onto one large one. As I did, I caught a glimpse of a large black snake slipping into the water. It happened so fast, I couldn't determine how long it was, but I did get the sense that the largest part of it was as big around as a coke bottle. Its head by contrast seemed quite small!

After exploring among the rocks (saw some empty clam shells), I saw the snake again and it looked to be about a yard long. A red-winged blackbird got very excited and approached a group of trees and bushes at one end of the island. I thought he might have a nest in there so I skirted that area so as not to excite him again. When I rowed away a little later, I saw him flitting from tree to tree, and I sensed he was proud of having vanquished me. Should I call it "Blackbird Island" or "Snake Island"?

The following day, I saw four swans flying low over the parking lot at Purdy's railroad station (about 20 miles south of the lake)—they were flying in formation about as high as a two-story house. Their wings moved so smooth and gracefully they seemed to be flying in slow motion.

> a cool breeze—
> somewhere in the lush garden
> it finds the windchimes

*

Three Birds

>   The Webhannet Marsh
>   in Wells, Maine
>   June & July 1981

a killdeer
on a sandy tideflat
in the Webhannet estuary
looking like a striped clown
or a miniature flying tiger
with his four black bands
across his face and breast (throat)
      bending over
      he spreads his tail feathers wide
      and gives a rippling call

            a greater yellowlegs
            on the same sand bar
            stalking regally into the water
            with stately circles rippling about him
            and then bobbing mechanically
            a few times

beautiful green heron
in marsh—misty morning
blueish green on top of his head
with white streaks on his light green or tan breast;
almost as plump as a grouse, yet larger
dark green back, glowing
blueish green, almost
luminous crown very
striking—

        from a windy ridge
        I hear the loon's call
        down on the lake

           *

Walking the Beach (Wells, Maine)

                                                  Friday, July 10, 1981

on the beach
near the water (low tide)
a mourning cloak butterfly
flutters close to me for a long time,
finally landing on the back of my right hand,
staying there as I walked about
thirty yards along the beach. Then
fluttering off, the tiny blue dots
near the edge of her wings
winking in the sunlight.

                        sunlit surf
           sandpipers whirl to another spot
                  far down the beach

                              *

The Wasp

June 2, 1982—NYC

Today I noticed the gall I'd kept under a glass since I broke it from a weed stalk a few weeks ago (May 5) on my hike in the woods near Lake Dutchess now had a small hole bored in it. And there perched on the inside of the glass was a small, brownish-black wasp with clear wings and two wiggling antennae on its head and with a large belly. The gall itself was as large as a robin's egg and was formed on the piece of weed stalk like a swelling.

I set the glass right-side up on an outside window sill, in the sunlight. This is a kitchen window looking out on St. Mark's churchyard where there are a lot of trees and bushes, including a horse-chestnut, whose leafy branches are only a few feet from this third-floor window.

The wasp, about the size of a medium-sized ant, walked about a little on the inside of the glass (a wine glass) and then stopped and preened its wings in the sunlight. After only about a minute, or less, it flew from one side of the glass to the other, climbed to the rim of the glass, hesitated for a split second and flew away—I lost sight of it almost immediately, it moved so fast. The air, the light, the sky, the yard, the world seemed so immense for this little creature to wing away into it so suddenly, to take its chances in life, so soon after emerging from the little space inside the gall—a swollen piece of weed stalk, the size of a small elongated cherry.

>   distant train —
>   a painted-lady flutters
>   in the garden

*

Joyful Things

From a Notebook—July 5, 1984

Three marvelously joyful things in the past few weeks: Lionel Hampton at Carnegie Hall with Illinois Jacquet and then Hampton's band again with Zoot Sims at Avery Fisher Hall.

Then the fireworks last night inciting me to shouts of delight with its sky full of lights above the East River, as Hampton had done with his halls full of swinging, torrentially exciting, soul-drenching sounds of happiness.

And then today the lonely wit and gentle poignancy, the deft artistry and irresistible charm of Charlie Chaplin in "The Idle Class" at the Public Theater.

Where else, all three in such a short space of time—but in New York!

And then even a lovely crescent moon high over the city—silently floating west after the fireworks.

The Rockettes The Rockettes The Rockettes

*

Fireflies

> East 10th Street, NYC
> Sunday—July 9, 1984

Walked by myself from Leigh's (on the Upper East Side) to Central Park a little after nine this evening. Very dramatic sky with large cumulous clouds scudding across the blue, then blue-black, then black sky—with the clouds becoming blacker on it—and a bright, luminous gibbous moon, with a slight aura surrounding it.

I went under some dark trees in the park, inside the 79th Street entrance, and watched the fireflies blinking in the darkness for a little while with the moon also shining through the trees from high over Fifth Avenue. Some of the fireflies were blinking quite high up among the tree branches—fifteen or twenty feet up—they would glow brightly suddenly, then dim out. It was lovely and quiet watching these little lights going on and off in that rich deep darkness held by the grasses and the dense tree leaves.

Back to Leigh's to say "good night" and then home.

July 13, 1984

Saw a firefly in the Saint Mark's churchyard from my third floor window Wednesday evening. It got dark early and as the sky darkened it began to thunder. It was about 8 PM. This one firefly lit up 6 times just outside the open window, high up in the branches of a sycamore tree (plane tree?). I could make out its trajectory as it lit and faded during its short flights. It was very pleasant to have such a light so close to home.

> rainy night
> lights shine from the backs
> of the sideshow tents

*

The Flying Seed?

June 29, 1986—NYC

The last few days I've seen a lot of downy seeds flying, floating and tumbling through the air around the city. They appear to be some kind of thistledown. The one whose adventure I am going to recount may have actually lost its seed, for where its filaments, or feathery fluff-like wings came together at the bottom to—I would assume—hold a seed: it appeared to be empty.

The night before last I was eating alone in a Thai restaurant on Broadway below 8th Street when I noticed this particular "seed" go floating slowly by my table—it must have come through the door earlier behind someone's shoulder. It slowed even more and settled to the red carpet. Afraid it might get stepped on and be smashed into the barren fuzz, I got up and rescued it, placing it in a deep cut-glass (clean) ashtray on my table.

I watched it while I ate my dinner. Each waving filament seemed to have tiny side branches, sort of plant-like, tiny white wisps off of tiny white wisps—like miniature bolts of energy or ghostly ferns. It seemed to never be completely still—some of the arms, or wings, were always waving if only slightly. At one point the whole "entity" spun like a moving top, rising up from the bottom of the ashtray. At another point it swept rolling to one side and climbed to the rim, perching on its edge as if readying to take its chance again in the world of space by lifting off into the air. I advised it with a thought, perhaps even a whisper, to wait a few minutes and I would take it outside and release it into the air above Cooper Union Square where it would have lots of space to take off and go in any direction it and the winds of chance or fate wanted it to go.

I took it by a few of its hands, or feelers, gently between the thumb and forefinger of my left hand and took it along to Cooper Union Square on my way home to 10th Street. Perhaps it could find a place to plant its seed, if it actually had one hidden somewhere.

However, it began to rain before we got there, and I assumed flight conditions would be poor—it might get soaked and flattened onto the pavement before it could plant anything. Besides, it might want to experience a soaring, exhilarating flight before beginning its metamorphosis into a plant. So I took it home with me. I left it on a small blue plate (anchored by a small matchbox leaning on a couple of tendrils) on the kitchen table, next to the window looking out on the bushes and trees of Saint Mark's west churchyard.

The thought came to me that I could ensure it a safe place to turn into a plant by planting it myself in a pot. It rested there all day while I thought about it.

Today is a beautiful warm, breezy day—and I'm sure it and I would be happier to be free. So I've just released it out the open window and it has risen almost straight up from my 3rd floor past the branches and leaves of a mighty (plane?) tree and has disappeared into the blue sky with my best wishes following it.

>	back road
>	a dragonfly cools off
>	on top of my aerial

*

The Click Bug, Etc.

September 11, 1986—after 11:00 PM

I can hear the click bug clicking in a tree—think in a tree—in the churchyard (Saint Mark's) just outside my window (on the 3rd floor). I call it a "click bug" because the sound it makes sounds like a loud click. There is a beetle called a click beetle, but I think that only makes a little click in its effort to turn itself over whenever it falls on its back. I don't know what this bug is called, but I've heard its song many times over the years in warm weather here in the city.

Sometimes it just gives one or two clicks, other times it gives a whole series—so that it sounds like a rattle, or a kid dragging a stick along a picket fence. I like it. It is as if nature is alive and pulsing in the night. (I've only noticed it at night.) The sound, though it is more sharp and clipped than a cicada's song, is somehow more intimate, too. Last year it (or another one) was in a tree someplace in front, along 10th Street. I used to hear it through the front window—this year it is somehow more mysterious, more powerful, speaking from the great tree and bush-scattered earth of the churchyard. I think there may be more than one tonight, because the sound is now coming from a different part of the yard.

I wonder—does it fly? Or is it a kind of cricket? It does not have the great peacefulness of a cricket's chirp. Though it seems a bit anxious, or excited, when it rattles. When it just clicks once or twice, it is as if it is asking a question. Sometimes the rattle may come almost as fast as a cicada's call.

I can remember the great songs of the katydids up at Lake Dutchess and the crickets among the Catskill Mountains or in the woods near the lake—chirping a lonely and solemn song from under the autumn leaves, a dark tone that seemed to welcome the dusk of evening. Part of the charm of the click bug is its mystery. I don't know what it is—maybe it is not even a bug! Also the simplicity of its sound—a click!

> sunset
> a spittle bug dreams
> among its bubbles

*

The Winter Wren

April 11, 1987—NYC

Went up to Central Park on my dinner "hour" from *Newsweek*—5:00 PM till 6:30 PM.

The cherries by the reservoir are all in blossom—very full, but not as lush as last year. Lots of forsythia still forsythifying bright yellow here and there.

Went up to the stream in the Ramble where all the bird-feeders are. Saw a beautiful little bird, very tiny, about as big as a small hen's egg, reddish-brown with a light fretwork of greyish-black mackerel-like markings, half underlying the russet and slightly overspreading it as the bird fluffed its feathers. It was ducking in and out of rocky declivities or under roots, etc. along the stream—very silent, as silent as the still waters, for the stream was not running.

Later after work about 10 PM ate at Shĭl-La, the Korean restaurant on Fifth about 30th Street. Had a great meal—hot codfish soup, sushi, five different vegetable appetizers, etc., couple of scotches (Dewars). Talked to Mrs. Kim, etc.

Walking home saw the full moon above the lit clock tower over Madison Square at 23rd Street.

> scudding clouds
> the full moon sails
> through them

*

Think the bird I saw in the Ramble, mentioned above, may have been a winter wren—but don't remember its tail sticking up! The bird guide also says it has a "heavily barred belly." I didn't particularly notice those markings on the bird I saw, but I was standing above it and couldn't see its belly very well. Perhaps that's what I glimpsed when he fluffed his feathers and wings. However, "he keeps close to the ground" seems to describe its actions for he went down into little cave-like holes under rocks, under overhanging banks, etc.

*

Sunday, May 3, 1987

Yesterday on my dinner hour (+ a half) from work 5 PM to 6:30 PM I went up to Central Park and walked around the Ramble where the lake inlets are near the Indian Cave and up on the hill where the stream is, looking for birds, especially the winter wren I saw a week or so ago.

Pretty sure I saw him again (or another one). He looked the same and he went through the same business of poking into holes and turning over small rocks. He was so busy, I forgot to notice if his tail stuck up or not! Also saw a myrtle warbler, a common yellowthroat warbler (with the black "mask"), red-winged blackbirds, several different kinds of sparrows, and lots of robins; even an immature one with a speckled (thrush) breast—how old could it be this time of year? It moved and acted just like a robin & looked like one, too, except for color and smaller size. And I may have seen some flycatchers. Day was partly overcast—apple blossoms about half-through, blossoms scattering—last of double pink cherries losing their petals, too. Young leaves bright yellows and greens. Horse-chestnuts, also—though their blossoms are poor this year compared to last.

The large poplars near the bridge (on the inlet towards the Delacorte Fountain) were pretty full with new leaves, which were fluttering brightly in the cool breeze.

Very pleasant jaunt.

*

The Katydid

129 East 10th Street, NYC

August 22, 1987 - Saturday night about 10:30 PM—just got home—a cricket was singing near the front door downstairs, among some weeds and flowers in front of the window to the side of the door, towards the churchyard—so close I tried to see him by lifting some of the leaning weeds to one side—but he stopped singing and I didn't see him. Then one of the click bugs started up over towards the church (in a tree?). After hearing the dark-voiced cricket, the click bug seemed a bit mechanical. The cricket also had a variety of musical tones and rhythms, as well as the nice voice.

August 23, 1987 - Sunday night almost 9:00 PM—just heard a katydid high in a blossoming pear tree a few doors west of here.

September 2, 1987 - Wednesday night about 10:30 PM—the 10th Street katydid is still at it. As I came home I heard him singing away more lustily than ever—seems in the willow oak on the south side of Tenth tonight.

September 3, 1987 - Thursday night about 11:30 PM—still (again?) in the willow oak—singing a little slower tonight.

September 7, 1987 - Monday (Labor Day) morning about 3:00 AM—it is raining slightly and the katydid is silent.

September 9, 1987 - Wednesday night after 11:00 PM—just got in, the katydid is still singing away—still in the willow oak. Has been a warm (75 - 80 degrees), humid, mostly sunny day. Tonight there is a gibbous moon (2/3 full) high in the east in a clear sky. Seems to be a lot of people "out on the town" tonight for some reason. Unusually so for a Wednesday night. Seems like a Friday or Saturday.

September 12, 1987 - Saturday morning 2:00 AM—when I got home about 12:30 AM the katydid was singing—still in the willow oak.

September 14 & 15, 1987 - Monday and Tuesday—still singing.

September 16, 1987 - Wednesday night 8:00 PM—still singing in the willow oak.

September 19, 1987 - Saturday night 8:00 PM—singing again, after being silent the last two (rainy) nights.

September 22 & 23, 1987 - Tuesday & Wednesday night 9:00 PM—katydid still singing—still in the willow oak.

September 26, 1987 - Saturday morning 12:45 AM (54 F - clear night)—just got home—no sound from the katydid—is it too chilly? Or too late?

September 26, 1987 - Saturday night 10:00 PM—warmer tonight 65 F—singing again, still in the willow oak.

September 28, 1987 - Monday night 9:30 PM - 74 F
—singing.

October 2, 1987 - Friday midnight—still singing.

October 4, 1987 - Sunday midnight—don't hear the katydid. The night is clear and cool - 48 F.

October 7, 1987 - Wednesday night about 8:00 PM—katydid singing, but voice not as loud as in the past, temp about 60 F—did not hear it last night, but can hear it now very faintly. I can only hear it now from my apartment if I open the window—did not open it last night, so couldn't hear him if he was singing as faintly then as he is now.

October 9, 1987 - Friday night 9:00 PM—just came in—katydid is not singing! Cool tonight 55 F.

October 15, 1987 - Thursday night 9:30 PM—just came in—have not heard the katydid for several days. It has been cool: 60's during day, 50's at night.

October 17, 1987 - Saturday night about 10:45 PM—just came in—still no sound from the katydid. Is he gone (stilled?) for good? 59 F.

[Or for the winter?!]

> a faint light
> off on a side road—
> rainy autumn night

*

The Pod

>October 26, 1987

The wisteria pod I picked in the Brooklyn Botanical Garden several days ago exploded on my living room table last night with a loud crack. I was in the kitchen. I had placed it under a small "tent" of folded paper so the seeds did not go far—about a foot and still on the table. The pod was now in two lengthwise halves. The noise was as if someone had struck the table with a long, supple stick, or switch, very hard—such as a hazel switch. It made me happy for some reason!

>a leaf
>drifts across the pond
>alone

*

The Duel

> January 26, 1993—Wells Beach, Maine

Earlier this week, went out for a walk to the bridge on the Mile Road to watch a pair of Goldeneye ducks, who were nesting somewhere near it. The Webhannet River runs under the bridge before it enters the ocean about a mile and a half further north. The temp was 22 F with bitter winds making it feel much, much colder.

This was my second day coming to watch the birds. Today the mate of the female bird was fighting and chasing away another male who had gotten too close to the female. He would fly along the top of the water splashing with his wings and sailing right at the intruder to chase him away. If he didn't go far enough away, then the attacking duck dove under him and came right up from beneath him, beak to the "fore" and goosed him, forcing him to jump into the air. After a few of these attacks, the beleaguered duck dove under the water. He was immediately followed by his determined foe and the battle continued underwater. Soon the chase continued on the surface in a flurry of wings, water and feathers until the perpetrator took off and flew to a distant part of the river's marsh and disappeared.

> autumn evening
> the roadside puddle
> grows still

*

Mergansers, Mergansers

April 17, 1994—Wells Beach, Maine

Very windy, sunny day today. Temperature in the high 50's F. Walked along the beach then up to the road by the old fire station, which fronts the cove there. The ocean washes up to piles of huge rocks, so there is no beach. You can stand on the side of the road, opposite the fire house, and look just over the rocks to a fairly deep and wide stretch of ocean.

I watched two groups of mergansers (red-breasted) fishing in the bay directly in front of me. It was between 12 and 1 in the afternoon. The tide was coming in. I had my father's binoculars with me and enjoyed watching the birds fishing, diving and swimming in the choppy waters for more than half an hour. I was standing on the side of the road (Webhannet) above the rocks below, where the tide was washing in (there was little or no traffic behind me). I had a good view.

There were two "pairs" of birds in one group of mergansers. And about 50 yards south of those, there was a group of three birds, two males and one female. Though the cove was a bit protected from the wind, there was enough to keep the water splashing around some and there were even a few waves breaking close to where the two pairs were fishing—about 50 yards straight out from me.

The black crests of the males fluttered in the wind and the birds were pictures of grace as they swept past each other or dived in tandem, sometimes looping into half circles as they entered head first into the water.

The females with their orange heads and crests were graceful, too, but they didn't have the flair of the males. The males were larger, also; and were more vividly marked with their colors of white and black. Their crests are larger, too, than those of the females. Their darkness against the sparkle and lightness of the dancing sunlit waves and foam was also very dramatic. As they sailed in and through the waves and when they swiftly turned to curve into a dive, neck, body, all quickly disappeared into the depths—it was like a magician's disappearing act.

At one point, one of the males cruised along the surface, his head in the water and his body stretched smoothly back of his out-stretched neck— he reminded me of a scuba diver looking down below the surface as his body was on top of it. The merganser wriggled slightly as he moved forward in this searching motion. He moved this way like a fish for 10 or 15 feet and then dove down after lifting his head briefly (to get air?). This was the first time I ever saw a duck surveying below the surface while swimming on top of it.

It was also interesting to see the foam flying from the waves, both breaking waves and rounded rollers whose tops were blown off into spray by the wind long before the waves actually broke.

starting to rise
to the top of the wave
the duck dives into it!

*

March 18, 2006—NYC

Pleasant walk to Stuyvesant Cove this afternoon, a brisk, cold, sunny day. The sun very bright on the East River, which was a silvery blue. Bright blue skies, too, with a few fluffy clouds. Saw seven red-breasted mergansers floating and fishing about thirty-five yards out. Had my binoculars with me, so was well prepared to view any show the birds might put on.

There were two males and five females. All were beautiful. Both sexes, besides the reddish breasts, have white collars and white wing markings. The males have glossy black heads and blackish-green crests; the females have red heads and crests. (Peterson's bird book describes the male as "rakish.") The wind was blowing their crests back and forth. The birds' colors and stream-lined shapes are both startling and striking.

Also saw an attractive pair of bufflehead ducks and a pair of American black ducks—but the star attraction was the platoon of mergansers.

summer
a kingfisher splashes in and
out of the river

Seven Haiga Sketches

Put me up the stairs
at the small mozzarella shop
autumn evening

The last streetlight
at the edge of town
turns upside

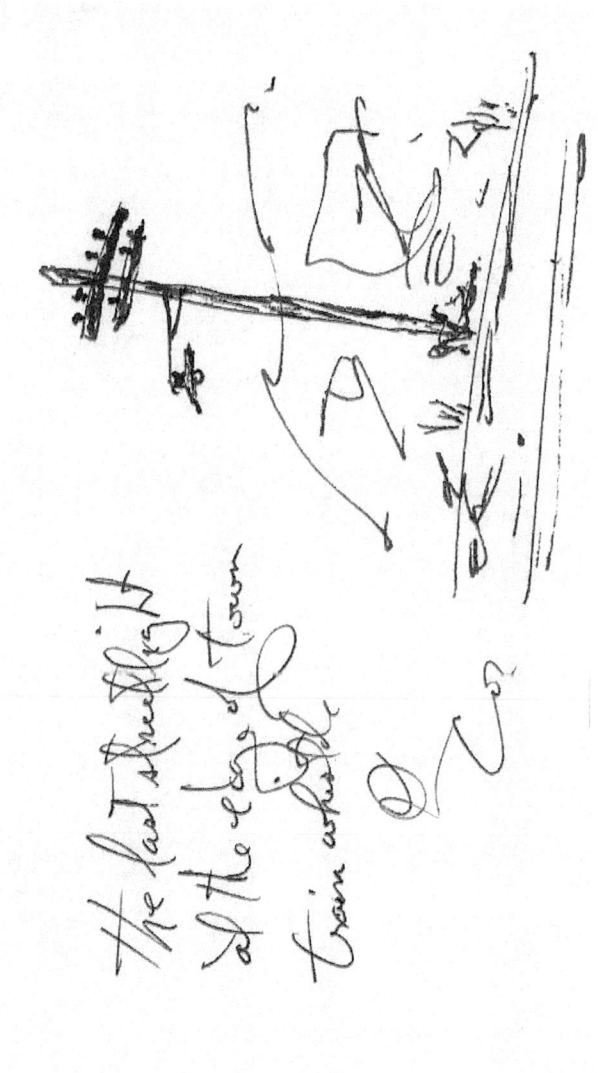

Late February —
Stuck to the tree, a snowball
in the strike zone

— Corman

while watering
the pot I met Tulips
I take a drink, too

winter sea
Through clouds to the sun shines
on two... one duck*

*bufflehead

PART B:

Haibun for Basho's Frog

Hitch-Hiking

It has been raining all day. I've been trying for a ride now for about two hours, walking with my backpack since my last ride dropped me off at a country crossroads six or seven miles back. Resting on the wooden post of a guard rail, I gaze into the dripping woods from under my small black umbrella. The young leaves glitter among the boles and limbs of the trees, which shine darkly in their wet-coated bark. An eighteen-wheeler whirls by, clouds of spray spinning from its wheels. The wind from its passing ripples a puddle by the side of the road. As the truck disappears around a far bend in the road, the puddle is quiet again. It is in a slight depression of the sandy-dirt shoulder of the road, between the black pavement and the grass and weeds at the edge of the woods. It's just a little further on from the last post of the guard rail, on which I'm sitting. The guard rail is here because of a brook that goes under the road and through the woods. In the puddle now are only the rippling circles from the raindrops falling in a slow drizzle. One raindrop startles a bubble into existence on the puddle. It floats a little way across the surface for a moment then vanishes. I shoulder my pack and continue on, walking on the soft shoulder of the road in my sneakers. The earth gently accepts each step and then gently lets it go.

After a few more miles it grows dark. I keep walking. The intermittent traffic becomes even more scarce. There are no houses or lights on the road. I am coming to an unlit intersection.

>distant truck
>the beads of glass light up
>on the STOP sign

*

The Last Streetlight

New York City
May 2001

A streetlight shines down a country road in autumn. From the highway it seems far off in the past. A faint glow off on a side road. The light hangs from near the top of a telephone pole. It is just a bare bulb with a flat-planed tin shade above it, a type of streetlight common back in the 1930s and '40s. The shade for these lights was a round metal plate with a slightly-angled tilt down from its center to its outer edge, like a small Japanese umbrella. It looked almost flat from a distance, but it was actually rippled. The ripples were not like circles from a stone dropped into a pond. They radiated straight out from the top of the bulb like rays from the sun. The shades were dark on top. The underside was painted with a white porcelain-enamel that reflected the light down to the street.

A metal rod holds the light to the telephone pole. The rod comes straight out horizontally from the pole, then curves up then down again so that the end fits vertically into the fixture on top of the shade: a small bell-shaped metal housing, really an extension of the shade itself, which contains the socket and wiring. The rod holds the light a few feet away from the pole so that it hangs out over the street or road. The pole might have only one wire strung on it. Or it might have a crossbar or two, each holding several wires. These crossbars are in relative darkness at night, for they are above the light. The telephone poles and their crossbars were never painted, and the natural wood lightened or darkened with the weather and with the passage of time. It might look light and silvery in the spring and summer sunshine or dark and greyish-brown in the rains of autumn and winter.

Such telephone-pole, or utility-pole, streetlights have a lonely look about them, particularly if they are on a back road, out in the countryside, or on a road through the woods—though they have some of this look wherever they are located. Except for the smaller towns, especially those that were hardly more than one or two stores and a crossroads, this bare-bulb-and-reflector streetlight was sometimes too plain for the center of town. A big city, or good-sized town, would usually use them only in poorer neighborhoods, in the factory and warehouse districts, or on the outskirts. In these more deserted areas, their loneliness was intensified by the lack or scarcity of other kinds of lights, such as those from stores or the lighted signs of restaurants and theaters. And the further away they were from the glitter of downtown, the further apart they were from each other. A bulb and shade on every third or fourth or even seventh or eighth telephone pole. Isolated spots in the darkness of night.

country road
a lone streetlight
in the rain

In many downtown areas and in the better residential neighborhoods, the streetlights or streetlamps had their own special poles and tended to be fancy and ornate, with globes hiding or softening the bulbs. Remnants, and restorations, of some of these more ornamental lights can still be seen across America. Many were done in turn-of-the-century art nouveau style. Such are the lampposts that still line the roads and pathways of New York's Central Park. The slender, yet pillar-like, dark metal poles extend at the top into several narrow tendrils of metal that curve around the white-glass oval-globes to hold them in place. As if a vine were growing over them. In recent years the city has put old-fashioned lamps on the streets around Manhattan's smaller parks, too, and on streets in historical districts. Some of these are the same simple straight ones you see in Central Park. Others, such as those around the little park in Abingdon Square, are taller wrought-iron poles shaped like giant Bishop's Crooks, with a large glass globe hanging from the end of each curved handle. A molded vine twines up and around each pole. They are painted black and look more Victorian than art nouveau.

Though impressive, giving a stately and warmly-dignified air to the neighborhood in spite of the cold streamlined, modern streetlights that are still nearby, these period lamps give only a suggestion of the opulently designed lampposts that decorated the downtown areas of many of our wealthiest cities in the 19th and early 20th centuries. Those old lampposts were often much larger and more elaborate. They had heavier poles, with fluted and embossed lines swirling around them. Some of them twisted from the decorated base up almost twenty or more feet into the air, narrowing at the top and curling over to support the hanging lights, great wrought-iron sconces in lozenge or box shapes with points like spearheads—or like those on a King's crown—sticking up all around each one, with writhing metal vines enclosing the frosted glass panels through which the electric light would glow. Sometimes there might be three or four, and even five, of these great torches suspended from, or supported by, one giant pole that branched out at the top. Even the simpler lights were impressive, such as the big white globes perched on high, straight, pillar-like columns set on classical pedestals. The globes, too, came in different shapes: acorn, oval, egg, spherical, box, octagonal, or lozenge; and in different types of glass: translucent, pebbled, frosted, clear, or white. The white globes stood out more in the daytime than the clear-glass ones, and at night they softened the glare of the bulbs.

Even the small city where I grew up in New Hampshire had decorative lights in the downtown area, though they had some telephone-pole lights there too. The most ornate lights were in front of city hall and the bank. The streetlamps in front of the bank were aided by two more large globes on great wrought-iron sconces set on flourishing metal brackets that leaned out from the front wall of the bank at both sides of the great metal doors of the entrance. At the public library, short bronze pillars on either side of the brick entranceway-stairs held more modest globes to light your way to the knowledge and wisdom that awaited you on the shelves and stacks within. The perfect white spheres were balanced and centered right on the top of their round, fluted pillars.

Such a small city or town would have a warm glow in the late evening from the lampposts that lined its streets. They, too, could take on a lonely, poignant look, a weathered timeless quality, evoking the past even when they were new. For the designs were adapted from the past, some from the old gaslights of the 19th century and others from even earlier times: from medieval and ancient elements and imitations of nature. In the center of town when other lights were on—store-window lights, neon signs, and the lights blinking from theater marquees and night clubs and restaurants—this effect would be largely lost in the glare. But if these were all out, most of them before midnight, the streetlight took on a soulful, distant wail of a saxophone look, and made your shadow on the sidewalk as you headed home from the just-closed bar seem like the last lost inhabitant of the world.

> the neon sign goes out
> from her hotel she looks down
> at the empty, wet street

These old lampposts sometimes give a sense of what Japanese haiku poets refer to as *sabi*, the loneliness of things, a loneliness tinted with the patina of time. However, most of them are too elegant or ornate. The bare-bulb-on-a-telephone-pole streetlight evokes *sabi* more readily. Its simplicity and crudity are like the old, cracked teabowls treasured in the tea ceremony. The bare wooden pole scarred with splintery holes from the climbing spikes that linesmen strapped to their boots, the bare bulb under its plain metal shade, even the wires stretching from pole to pole, have the practical bareness of utility and simplicity, essential elements of *sabi*. When surrounded by the blackness of night, these lights shine with an austere, yet profound loneliness.

Modern streetlights don't evoke the melancholy feeling of the old lights. The new cobra lights look cold and mechanical. Encased in their thick ridged-glass globes, these gleaming spaceship-headlights lean out over the street on their long slender curved steel poles like snakelike aliens from another planet. They emit a phosphorescent glare that turns the street into a stark and empty nightmare.

The plain bulb on a telephone pole, despite its crude simplicity or perhaps because of it, has a charm that may not be so different from that which the old gaslights of the 19th century have for some people. Each creates its own kind of lonely atmosphere: that of the telephone-pole light is high and cool, the gaslight close and warm. All the different kinds of illumination the human race has used through the ages, from ancient torches and watch fires to candles and oil lamps, to the streetlights of our own century, have an emotional effect on our sensibilities.

For someone who grew up with telephone-pole streetlights, they can evoke more intense feelings of loneliness than any other kind, though you rarely see them anymore except in old movies. As a boy, I lived most of the time outside of town, in the country. There were still a few small working farms in our area. Though our road, the Old Rochester Road, was mostly residential, many of the houses were separated by fields or woods. I did a lot of walking, or riding my bike, home in the dark and often the only things to light my way were the streetlights, which were quite far apart on the roads outside of town. If on my bike, there was also the narrow beam of light from the small lamp on my front fender.

In my teens and twenties, while going to college, in the service, or just traveling across America, I did a lot of hiking and hitchhiking. I would find myself on a highway or road in the Kittatinny Mountains in Pennsylvania or the Cascade Mountains in Oregon, standing under a lonely streetlight with my thumb pointing down the road, hoping to get a ride. I had plenty of time while walking from one light to another to dream about the things to see and do when I reached San Francisco or Seattle: the people I would meet and the poems I would write. And time to think about the different kinds of lights there are in the world and in the universe and about the darkness that is around us.

> deserted crossroads
> by the closed filling station
> a streetlight comes on

When in the Air Force in 1950 stationed in Panama City, Florida, I used to hike and hitchhike into Pensacola and once even up to Mobile, Alabama. Passing old wooden shacks with dim lights in the windows, I'd walk along the dark roads with only an occasional patch of light from a streetlamp to guide my way. Then in 1958 on my way back from my pilgrimage to San Francisco's poetry scene—where I discovered Japanese haiku after hearing Gary Snyder mention it at a gathering of poets, which included Robert Duncan and Jack Spicer, in George Stanley's North Beach apartment—I was hiking and hitching on a road through a desert on my way from the Grand Canyon to the Billy the Kid Museum in Fort Sumner, New Mexico. Here there were no streetlights at all. Just the darkness and the stars. Once in a while, the distant lights of a ranch house. Still using my old Air Force duffel bag to carry my stuff in, I sat on it at the side of the road while waiting for a ride, and played a harmonica that I had recently bought and was teaching myself to play. I'd been dropped off by a cowboy in a pickup truck who had turned into a dirt road leading to a ranch so far off there was no sign of it except for the barbed wire fences strung along the road. I played "Camptown Races."

Hitching to Seattle from Maine a few years later, I spent many nights on city streets and country roads all across America, standing under streetlights with my thumb out for a ride. Often the only lights were the headlights of the passing cars. In North Dakota I tried riding on railroad freight cars for a while, sometimes seeing the lights on distant roads through the open doors of the rattling boxcar. I got back on the road after a few hundred miles, for riding the rails was too dirty and even dangerous. I remember getting out of my boxcar hideout in a switching yard in some city and running across the tracks, which were gloomily lit by the stark lights of the yard. Lights that were high up on iron trestle-like frames far above the railroad signal lights. While the cars were being shunted around, I bought some cheese and crackers in a small grocery store and raced back to my boxcar.

In Seattle I lived a short while in a small two-room house set alone between a thruway and the railroad yards. It had been practically abandoned. There were only a few square feet of yard within the concrete abutments around it. It was alone in a sea of asphalt, floodlit by great phosphorescent highway lamps. I covered my few windows at night to keep out the light. There was always the sound of cars and trucks swirling around the house. Very late at night it was less steady and in the intervals I could hear the making up of freight trains down in the railyards. The house had only a few sticks of furniture, stuff that had been left there by previous tenants. I used an old washbasin as the shade to my only lamp, a bronze table-model shaped like a miniature streetlamp. Later I moved to the top floor of a three-story rooming house on top of Firewatch Hill, in a neighborhood of old family mansions. At night I'd watch, through the window just over my poem-littered desk, the ferry's twinkling rows of lights appear from out of the black mass of the Olympic Peninsula. It looked like a lit brooch moving over the vast darkness of Puget Sound towards me and Seattle.

> back road through pines
> night rain drips from the trees
> and a utility-pole wire

Drifting into late autumn, I walk again down a country road in a drizzly, cold rain with no light in the wet darkness except a lone streetlight. It's a long walk along the puddle-strewn shoulder of the road till the road bends around a long curve and the streetlight is lost behind a tangle of pines and nearly-bare hardwoods dripping and sighing with the sounds of wind and rain. In the distance ahead there's the glow of the next light along the road. It is haloed by the mist and rain that surround it. As we come closer we see that a circle of drops, almost a pouring stream, continually falls from the edges of the metal reflector the light wears like the rippled skimmer of a hat.

The dark house just beyond this solitary streetlight seems to be waiting for Humphrey Bogart to pull into its muddy driveway in that small coupe he drove in *The Big Sleep*. But nobody comes. There is nobody but me. And you, the night, the rain, and the streetlight.

dark farmyard
a streetlight by the driveway
shines from a puddle

In a snowstorm, a streetlight has a special kind of loneliness, a sort of purified solitude. As I stand by the side of the road watching this one, the falling snow seems to come out of nowhere to appear in its cone of light. Moving back, I can see the steadily falling snow settling slowly down on and around it, piling up on the crossbars of the pole and even creating round caps of snow on the pole's top and on top of the lightbulb's shade-reflector. And there are little mounds sticking above the snowy crossbars, too, covering the glass insulators that hold the wires. The night advances, the snow piles up, all traffic disappears. The road becomes impassable to vehicles, and the only sound is the whisper of the falling snow. The loneliness increases. A loneliness stretching whitely under the streetlight and around it in the air. It goes off into the gray darkness beyond the light, and then into the shadowy invisible blackness of the night. And still the flakes of whiteness fall. Endlessly falling out of—and into—this loneliness.

> after the snowfall
> the road's gone and there's
> only the white woods

On a night in spring a streetlight illuminates at the edge of its circle of light a few blossoming petals on a branch of an apple tree. Only one branch leans into the light but the whole flowering tree looms whitely in the shadows beyond. And still beyond that is the orchard spreading a giant, ghost-like cloud of blooms far into the night. And high above, real clouds from a recent shower scud across the starry sky.

A streetlight at the corner of a vacant lot provides the light for a game of baseball that starts after supper and goes on into the evening until the cries of one or two mothers ring through the neighborhood calling their boys in to homework or bed. Since the outfield is nearly pitch dark, the game is played mostly on the infield and everyone bats opposite-handed.

Summer. And the streetlights are surrounded by insects. In town and in the country, moths bang into and circle the lighted bulbs. Different kinds of late-hatching mayflies and strange bugs with gossamer wings and long dangling legs or tails and even some with horn-like antennae rearing from their heads all pass in and out of the light. In the fields or in dark vacant lots, the crickets and cicadas sing through the warm night. Cooler nights, the cicadas take a rest and leave the stage to the crickets. Or maybe a chorus of a few thousand katydids will cover the treetops and roar their song up to the stars rolling along like a river above the river.

> from the long grass
> around a telephone pole
> a cicada's cry

On a country road a boy walks home from a regular game of baseball, his bat over his shoulder, his fielder's glove dangling from it. As he passes under one of the far-spaced streetlights, he hears the sound of a whippoorwill coming from the woods near the edge of a meadow and stops to listen. After a while he tries to imitate it, trying out several keys, then gives up and starts walking again, noticing how his two shadows fade and then appear again—behind him as he approaches a streetlight, and in front of him as he passes under it and moves away again. Every once in a while he will stop, put his bat down, and throw the ball straight up into the darkness and catch it in his glove as it comes back down. Now he turns into a dirt driveway and heads for the back door where a small light next to it lights the steps. As he opens the door there is the sound of a woman's voice. The door closes and we are alone on the road with only the next streetlight awaiting us.

Neon lights have had a more dramatic impact on the world around us than the changes in streetlights, especially in the way they have transformed some of our cities into riots of color. But they can also create an atmosphere of excitement or mystery, even danger, in suburban or rural settings. A neon sign on top of a small roadhouse way out in the country can suggest a film-noir scenario. Inside, an intrigue is developing that in its intensity carries the ominous threat of violence and even murder. A squad car will come flashing out of the highway darkness at any minute to answer a call to the police about a lurid and terrible homicide.

Or we may find a lighted sign on an otherwise deserted mountain road. There is one, just ahead, for a cocktail bar in that large resort hotel. The sounds of jazz emanate from somewhere in the interior and float out into the summer night, filtering into the nearby woods. The neon sign, in the shape of a cocktail glass with a blinking swizzle-stick, glows by the side of the road. The glass is in the triangular shape of a martini glass, set on its long stem and its flat circular base. It is slightly tilted to give a sense of movement, of excitement. A sense that things may shift out of control. That we may dance recklessly into a romantic but dangerous love affair. One that is illicit and may turn violent.

> the jukebox swirls
> with color and a Basie tune
> the pinball machine tilts

Out in the country—or even in a deserted part of the city—a neon sign by itself sets a mood of loneliness. Any suggestion of excitement or good cheer it may have is tinged with sadness and even a trace of suspicion. For the lone sign—however bright—is surrounded by the darkness and space of a night world that holds a threat of the unknown. It pulses with the mystery and even the menace of nature—and the abnormal. In the entertainment sections of a big city, there are bright lights in enough profusion and variety to allay, or temporarily hide, our fears of what might lurk in the dark. There all the lights gather together in a great blaze of praise to the joys of eating, drinking, music, dancing, sex, and romance.

Thousands of bulbs in marquees—for theaters, dance halls, striptease joints, and nightclubs—race back and forth in high-speed synchronization, going off and on in split-second rotation, so that the light seems to be racing around the perimeter of each sign, whirling as if gone mad. Neon signs in the shapes of crescent moons or stars or palm trees or bubbling glasses of champagne flash off and on in all the colors of the rainbow. There is a martini glass with a neon nude sitting in it in place of the swizzle stick. The lights flicker back and forth so that she kicks her legs into the air. Here is a tuxedoed figure in a top hat beckoning you in with his neon cane. There are all kinds of lit-up signs for restaurants, bars, and hotels. Closed stores keep their signs on and their windows lighted to show off jewelry, furs, automobiles, cameras and television sets. Even in the five-and-ten-cent store on the next corner, hidden lights toss their frozen glitter among the assorted ephemera in the windows.

All this flashing and blinking, blazing and flaring of lights at last comes to an end. After midnight or one or two a.m. they will begin to dim and go out and even the most sophisticated city street can get a lonely and desolate look from a single blinking bar sign. And a rainy night down by the waterfront—where there are still cobblestone streets with a single bar open at two or three in the morning with its small neon sign winking on and off or just glowing steadily with the words "BEER ON TAP" under the drizzling neon rain and reflecting its light in the wet and streaming cobblestones and with the lapping sounds of the river only a few feet away in the darkness—can sweep through you with all the wistful longing of a song by Billie Holiday. We can almost hear the evanescent notes of Lester Young's answering solo.

But when these last little signs go out at three or four in the morning, there are still the streetlights. They will burn on until dawn begins to lighten the skies. As the morning sun tries to lean through the cloudcover of the still drizzling heavens, enough of its light filters through to at last put them out. The neon sign is dark and dusty in the window of the bar and, as you walk along the wet sidewalk, there is only the faint hiss of the rain and a cold wind flaps the hanging edge of a canvas awning that has been left out over the front of a pawn shop.

Along the waterfront the river is gray and metallic with a few whitecaps curling up in a fitful wind. The sky lightens—but the sun is still obscured by mist and clouds. It's a new day. The neon, the music, the laughter are waiting, ready to start up again. Soon there will be another night. The city will greet it with a million lights.

Out in the countryside there are still lonely places that hold back the night with only a lone streetlight. As the twilight gathers and deepens and rain darkens the wood of its telephone pole, the bulb flickers on. Drops of rain glisten on the splinters that stick out from the small holes in the pole. They fall and are replaced. A truck goes by. As it fades into the distance, its tires throw up clouds of mist that glow in the taillights.

> the last streetlight
> at the edge of town
> train whistle

*

Stepping Up To The Bar

...he looked around with a slow smile of pleasure.

"I like bars just after they open for the evening. When the air inside is still cool and clean and everything is shiny and the barkeep is giving himself that last look in the mirror to see if his tie is straight and his hair is smooth. I like the neat bottles on the bar back and the lovely shining glasses and the anticipation. I like to watch the man mix the first one of the evening and put it down on a crisp mat and put the little folded napkin beside it. I like to taste it slowly. The first quiet drink of the evening in a quiet bar—that's wonderful."

I agreed with him.

—Raymond Chandler
The Long Goodbye

Dropped into Swift's pub on East 4th Street off the Bowery the other day for a black and tan (Guinness stout and Bass ale) and found myself admiring the wood bar, particularly the bar's foot-rail, which is not actually a rail. It's a small wooden platform that runs along the front of the bar and is attached to its base. It extends seven inches out from the bar and is about the same number of inches high. "J.P." Doran, the young Irish bartender, said such a wooden-platform type of "rail" is common in Ireland, especially in the older pubs. I asked him what it was called and he replied, "That thing you put your foot on." I suggested "footrest." "Foot-platform?"

Whatever it is it's a comfortable place to put a foot while leaning against the bar, passing the time of day, and drinking a frothy glass of stout and ale. After drinking about a third of my pint, I asked J.P. for another glass, empty, as is my custom, so I could pour the brew back and forth one or two times to put a head back on it, as I love to wet my moustache in the creamy suds as I drink my beer or ale.

Swift's is named for Jonathan Swift, the Irish satirist, who is most famous for writing *Gulliver's Travels*. There are title pages from his numerous books mounted in a glassed case on the wall and a mural depicting the great man in his study. Built out from the wall opposite the bar, there are standup bar-like tables with the same type of foot-platform running along below them.

> at the White Horse
> raising a glass to Dylan Thomas
> and the autumn moon

The next night I found myself in Greenwich Village at the Tavern on Jane Street, which is at the corner of Seventh Avenue. It has a beautiful, simple wooden bar. I noticed a footrest similar to that at Swift's and asked the bartender, Michael Stewart, who it turned out is one of the owners, what he called it. He said it was called a "step." He should know, he designed the bar himself.

The top, face, and step of this bar are all of oak. They are stained a dark mahogany color. The raised outside edge of the top, the bar rail, is mahogany. It is rounded with a wave or dip in it. I imagine it has several purposes: to keep glasses and bottles from slipping off the bar, to give patrons extra space to lean an elbow, and to provide a rounded support to grasp with one hand while raising a glass, or gesturing and expostulating, with the other. A narrow shelf set down about an inch on the bartender's side of the bar gives him a place to set things momentarily before placing them on the actual top in front of the thirsty customer. It is called the lip of the bar. My proclivity for extra glasses usually brings the lip into active service. I placed my right foot trustingly up on the step and ordered one of the tavern's carefully drawn black and tans—with my usual spare glass for keeping a frothy head on it. In general, I like an array of glasses in front of me. When I'm drinking scotch or bourbon, which I do more often than ale or beer, I like to have it on the rocks with an extra rock-glass filled with ice on the side, plus a highball glass of ice water to pour a splash from. I have my own miniature bar to play with.

Some Japanese bars minister to this whim of mine by providing me with a small silver ice-bucket, with tongs, and a matching pitcher of ice water. I guess I am not unique or they wouldn't have these things available. (Some Tokyo bars will even put the bottle of whiskey in front of you like in an old-time cowboy movie.) I took my time enjoying the black and tan, which I do with all my drinks. There are some things you just don't want to rush. After a Jack Daniel's on the rocks, with all the serious attention a good drink deserves, I wandered into the night.

> rainy afternoon
> alone at the bar listening
> to a distant ballgame

    Sometimes a step or foot-rail can be at the wrong level. The brass foot-rail at the old Fat Tuesday's on Third Avenue was just right (my foot rested there a number of times over the years, usually for a nightcap after listening to Maxine Sullivan or Dizzy Gillespie downstairs), but the one at the Knickerbocker on University Place is too high for me. I feel off balance. The small, cozy bar is in a corner of the restaurant by the windows and has only about a dozen stools, so a high rail seems especially out of scale. When I was there a few nights ago, I perched on a stool to get away from the awkward foot-rail, putting my feet on the front crossbar of the stool's legs. The top of the bar is marble with a raised wooden rail along the outer edge. I sipped my Dewars on the rocks and then placed my glass carefully back on the marble next to my other two glasses and proceeded to troll out a line about foot-rails to the bartender, Al. I was rewarded with some interesting information about a bar that used to be in the South Street Seaport. It had a heated foot-rail. The place, called the Paris Cafe, was open all night and was, according to Al, popular with workers from the fish market, especially during the winter months. He didn't know how it was heated. If it was metal perhaps it had steam running through it like a radiator.

> ice fishing
> feeling the fish nibble
> somewhere far below

I enjoy all the comforts of a good bar. Not only the physical amenities, but the psychological and spiritual as well. A bar can have different atmospheres of good cheer. From a muted and calm atmosphere to one filled with excitement and high spirits. It can depend on the people there or just the time of day or week. But the material aspects of the bar provide the foundation for your good time whether that consists of a quiet, contemplative drink or a bubbling, celebratory get-together with friends. I like a comfortable bar stool, preferably with a back. If the seat is not padded at least let it be concave to fit that curve most of us sit with. The bar and stool and step (or rail) should all be in proportion to fit the average customer. I want my feet to be happy, as well as my backside, and not be pestering me with unease when I'm trying to enjoy myself. When standing at the bar, my foot should find the step or rail at a comfortable position to rest on.

    I like the look of all the bottles lined up and lit up against the mirror behind the bar. I like the natural wood and sturdy stability of the traditional bar, a non-rocking ship sailing into the night. I even like all the glasses, sinks, and paraphernalia along the back. The different fruits and mixes that go to make the drinks, the bartender shaking a martini, the silver sparkle of the speed rack, or the well, where the bar brands, or well brands, are kept. I like bars in the afternoon when there is a quiet expectancy for what the evening and night might bring in the way of excitement, intrigue, or romance. I like them very late at night when there is a sad, bittersweet loneliness about them. How you feel in a bar depends a lot on how the bar itself looks and feels. But whether you have a pleasant bar experience or not is ultimately in the hands of the captain of this ship, the bartender.

<pre>
         by the Statue of Liberty
     our sailboat turns into the wind
         a rainbow in the spray
</pre>

    The following afternoon I was on the Upper West Side and ambled into O'Neals' on 64th Street off of Broadway for some refreshment. There were a pair of entertaining young men tending bar. Gaetano, who with his earring looks like Errol Flynn in one of those pirate movies, and Michael, who claimed to be the son of the deceased owner, Patrick O'Neal, the famous actor. Michael jokes around a bit and it is difficult to sort the blarney from the baloney. (Actually, there is a real Michael O'Neal, Patrick's brother, who is a part-owner with Patrick's wife, Cynthia, and Jim Enzel. Before Patrick's death in 1994, the place was known as The Ginger Man and there is a story about that, too, but we have to get back to our main subject.)

Gaetano knows a girl in Colorado who told him about a lodge there that has heated stones under the front of the bar so the skiers can warm their stockinged feet after a day on the frozen slopes. She didn't tell him how it was done. Could it have been adapted from the heated stones used in Indian sweat lodges? Or the heated bricks our ancestors took to bed with them? Heated in a fire and then placed under the bar? While we worried this hot topic, I cooled off with a black and tan.

O'Neals' has an ornate wooden bar with dark wood carvings and scrollwork along the walls and around the bright mirrors. Its brass foot-rail is just high enough for most people, including yours truly. The top of the bar has a raised wooden rail along the outer edge and about five inches below it there is a narrow brass rail that sticks out a couple of inches and, according to Gaetano, is there to hold your cane or umbrella if you should have one. It is also handy if you should feel a bit tipsy and need to grab hold of something. He learned these things from his father, who was a bartender. His father also told him he remembers brass spittoons, and that they were placed outside of the foot-rail so when a tobacco chewer spit into them, he could, hopefully, avoid hitting the rail or someone's foot, including his own. However, I've seen an old sepia print of a western bar which shows spittoons inside the rail. Perhaps in Tombstone if they were out in the open they were in danger of being kicked over by a listing cowboy or of attracting the attention of his six-shooter.

> from a window near the bar
> the evening sun glows in the snow
> on top of Blackfoot Mountain

At twilight O'Neals' has a nice custom of putting thick two-inch high candles in clear glass cups all along the bar, one to a stool. The flickering flames reflect from the polished wood and shine in the mirrors, evoking an earlier age of simple elegance. This was time for me to try some single malt scotches. From a sampling menu I chose Cragganmore, Laphroaig, and Lagavulin. All excellent. Laphroaig I took with some water as is recommended on the bottle itself: "adding water will release a rich aroma of peat smoke with some sweetness and strong hints of the sea."

Actually, after sipping a little of each from the large shot glasses, I tried them, with a little splash of water, on the rocks. Yes, three more glasses, with ice, and a fourth with ice water to be my pitcher. In clinking, tinkling, sparkling Glory. I also had a couple of delicious appetizers at the bar with my drinks: asparagus with sliced almonds and seared tuna with arugula and mâche. Asked what this last ingredient was, Michael informed me with an almost straight face that it is a rare fern that only grows beneath the apple trees of a remote region of the German Alps.

I should mention that I had a large white-linen napkin spread open on the bar for a tablecloth while I was eating at O'Neals'. My wife and I fairly often eat dinner at the bar instead of at a table. We've done it at the Gotham, the Union Square, and several other nice restaurants. We enjoy the informality, the chance to meet people, or to talk with the bartender. If the bartender doesn't think to spread a napkin, I ask for an extra one and spread it myself. The first time I remember having dinner at a bar where the bartender set everything up like this was at Raoul's in Soho quite a few years ago. I felt much more special and a part of the general festivities than I would have sitting alone at a table. I still remember what I had: a great steak frite with a couple of Johnnie Walker Blacks on the rocks. My feet were so comfortable I don't remember noticing them at all, so I'm sure Raoul's has a fine step or rail, though I don't remember which.

There are many ways to be innovative when designing something even so seemingly simple as a bar. There's a bar in Chicago with a heavy, glass top with rows of lights shining up from under it. Your drinks are illuminated. There are bars with zinc tops or slate tops. Bars with tile tops and even tile steps. One New York restaurant with a nautical theme has the whole bar, including the step, covered with heavy grey sheet metal studded with rivets. There is a country and western bar with a railroad tie for a step. In Florida, I saw a blue-tiled bar with a bamboo bar rail along the top. It had a matching tile step and padded, wicker-backed-and-armed barstools. There were real palm trees arching over each end of the bar.

glittering on the water
in the reeds at the swamp's edge
alligator knobs

    I remember many years ago in San Francisco being impressed with how the night clubs and bars were lighted. Some of them were bathed in subtle, muted tones of blue and gray to set a romantic film-noirish mood, while others were lit with lurid reds and yellows, suggesting a sexy pulp-fiction cover. The colors and lights were often augmented by matching sounds of jazz. In the blue bars, the music often emanated from a lone, cigarette-hanging-from-the-lip pianist. If they had a trio, the drummer rarely switched from his brushes. The more gaudy clubs would likely have a hot-jazz combo. Some places would swing both hot and cool. Back in the '50s, when I was a young airman just back from Okinawa, many of the bars in the Bay area still had no air-conditioning and the doorway, under a neon sign shaped like a martini glass, would be open to the summer night. The dark lights and tinkling jazz would draw us in from the sidewalk, especially if we glimpsed a blonde sitting alone at one end of the bar, the gleam of her crossed nylons shining like a beacon from the barstool.

> long-ago night, Jack Kerouac
> watches as the film crew lights Joan
> on foggy Russian Hill

A day or two after my visit to the Upper West Side, I happened to be at the Yardley Inn in Yardley, Pennsylvania. This is an inn dating to colonial times when it was called The White Swan. It became a favorite watering hole for bargemen on the Delaware River. I walked into the taproom to have a drink at the charming old circular wooden bar. The bar makes a perfect circle except where it joins the back wall. Even before getting up to the bar I could see it had a very unusual step. It was red. It was made of bricks. Three bricks high. The bricks of the top layer, on this attractive and, as I soon discovered, solidly comfortable step, are layed with one end against the bar, narrow side up, the other ends radiating straight out. The bricks in the lower two layers are layed the usual way parallel to the bar. Perhaps this unusual step was built to withstand the floodwaters of the river, which have at times found their way into the inn.

On this same trip to the lower reaches of the Delaware, my wife and I had brunch with her father at the King George II Tavern in Bristol, Pennsylvania, which is on the river just above Philadelphia. The tavern was built in 1681, the year Bristol was established. Perhaps it was the first building to be erected. We were told that George Washington had placed his buckled shoe upon the brass foot-rail of the tavern's bar in 1776. Someone else was sure that the Father of Our Country during that momentous year would, even while relaxing with a drink, have been wearing riding boots, not to mention his sword and pistol, to be ready for action against the British. This reminded my father-in-law of a story about the famous gunfighter and marshal, Wyatt Earp, who helped tame the Wild West of Dodge City. It seems that Earp, having had to take some action himself in a saloon with no foot-rail, put his spur-jingling boot on the neck of the villain he'd just shot, while he had a well-deserved shot of whiskey at the bar.

> at the bar raising a glass
> to an engraving of Washington
> kneeling in the snow

The next day while preparing to return to New York by train from Trenton, New Jersey, my wife and I stopped for a late lunch at Pete Lorenzo's Restaurant, which is just across the street from the train station. It is a wonderful old restaurant with all the polished wood and brass, ornate lamps and faceted-glass mirrors, the relaxed ease and comfort of the late nineteenth century. It has one of the most beautiful bars I've ever seen. We had been there several times before.

The first time, some years ago, we were told it was a place where politicians and Captains of Industry congregate to eat and drink. Just arrived by train from New York, we were having a drink at the bar while waiting for my wife's parents to pick us up. We told the bartender that we knew a Captain of Industry. My father-in-law owns his own engineering firm which for half-a-century has been doing work for the Navy. So when he and my mother-in-law arrived to pick us up, we invited them to have dinner with us there and ever since we've made a point of trying to visit Lorenzo's whenever we are in Trenton.

During this most recent visit, given my new interest in bar and foot-rail lore, I examined the bar with a more careful, and admiring eye than heretofore. But first we had a delicious antipasto and a few other delicacies to eat right at the bar. With these my wife had some wine and I had a Samuel Adams Boston Lager. Then, as it was late afternoon and there were only a few men left at the bar, and they at the other end, I ordered a single malt scotch, Bunnahabhain, and asked the bartender, Mike Kelly, if it was all right to light up my Macanudo cigar. He assured me it would be everyone's pleasure for me to do so. I lit up, enjoyed the tastes and aromas of both burning leaf and dew of the heather, and looked about me, feeling like a monarch surveying his kingdom. The bar is a gleaming cherry mahogany, with an outside bar rail about three inches in diameter set an inch away from the bar itself. It is of the same beautiful rosy wood and invites your elbows to lean on it and your hands to caress it.

At the bottom of the bar where we tend not to explore except with our feet, I found a little world of convenience. Closest to the foot of the bar was a small decorative step, or molding, of some kind of masonry, cement or plaster. Below this and extending five inches below the barroom floor itself was a tiled trough that extended the length of the bar and was equipped with a drain at one end. This came out from the step about five inches, and raised above its outer perimeter was a gleaming brass rail for your feet. Since the bartop extended out quite far, with an ample overhang, there was plenty of room underneath for all this. And your feet, or foot, could be comfortably tucked on the rail. A generous overhang on the patrons' side is an important element for any bar. Without it, when you sit on the barstool, you will find your knees bumping the front of the bar.

Extending out on the floor from the foot-rail for about a foot and a half, and running all around the L-shaped bar, is a pattern of white and colored tiles, making an elegant space to stand or position your stool on. The comfortably backed barstools have crossbars at a convenient spot on the legs, as do all sensible barstools, where you can also rest your feet. This allows you to reposition your legs several ways without getting off the stool. However, I always like to spend part of my time at a bar standing up, moving one foot then another onto the rail or step.

After hearing some of the history of the bar, including tales about important old-time politicians, prohibition-era gangsters, and other interesting characters who have frequented Pete Lorenzo's over the years, we said goodbye to Mike and headed across the street for our train.

> from the bar car lounge
> glimpsing a small town where
> the last movie is getting out

You don't realize how essential to enjoyable drinking a step or foot-rail is until you are standing at a bar and lift your foot up to find there is nothing there. (I've encountered a few such bars in New York.) The whole world seems out of balance and your legs become restless and awkward. You shuffle your feet and one of them lifts up searching again and again even though it knows it is useless. It's as if a horse were prevented from cocking up a hoof (usually a back one) onto the tip of his shoe while waiting harnessed to a carriage outside the Plaza Hotel. He'd get restless, stamp and fume, then neigh and rear in his traces. Probably become a wild-eyed, frothing-at-the-mouth runaway. So here's to the man who thought up the step and rail. Lift a foot up onto it, as you raise your glass.

*

Curbstones

A cool warm March wind blows off the East River and along a side street near New York City's South Street Seaport. The morning sun is coming out again after a spell of grayness. The light flows up the street, shines on the curbstone at my feet, flickers faint shadows along its irregular surface, and suddenly awakens within me the realization that I am once again in love.

Each spring I fall in love with granite curbstones. These natural-looking, rough-cut stones with their slightly rippled surfaces, their precise and monolithic solidities lining and defining a street from here to infinity, have for me the mysterious presence of mountains, the strange, halted stillness of great glacial deposits: at once both stopped and journeying—waiting millenniums, yet instantaneously moving through space with their star, our star.

Some granite curbstones have smooth tops—not polished, but simply flat as if planed. These have an artificial look and sunlight is washed out on them. On the more common, rough-hewn curbstone, the light is varied and soaks the stone with its magic, playing with shadows and intensities. On rainy days small pools form here and there along its top while the gutter stream flows below. The stone is closer to nature—wild and alive.

> waterfront bar
> the cobblestones glow
> in the night rain

    I grew up among the granite landscapes and seascapes of Maine and New Hampshire. From the mountains of New Hampshire and from rocky, mist-shrouded islands off the Maine coast have come the foundation stones of many of our towns and cities—for buildings and bridges, for statues and memorials, for cobblestones and curbstones. Still seen on little streets near the Boston and New York waterfronts are granite cobblestones, many of which were quarried from Maine islands. There is a stillness about them on chilly, rainy days in spring or autumn that suggests such origins. Wet and streaming like the rocky islands they were carved from, they call up a vision of the Atlantic splashing up against lonely shores, the sun coming out to shine on great, wet rocks gleaming amidst the desolate reaches of the rolling sea. For a hundred or more years, these cobblestones have been dusted and smeared with the grime of the city and washed again and again with sunlight and rain. Worn smooth like pebbles on a shore, they still have an unevenness that endears them to me.

    Curbstones, with much of their mass hidden in the earth below the pavement, rise above the street and show the way. Though still beneath our feet, they can be guideposts to where and how we direct our steps. Witnessing with a calm impassivity our rushing about from here to there, they also stand as monuments to the peace and wisdom that come from being still.

> fallen leaves
> the wind uncovers
> a granite curbstone

When I was a boy, curbstones were just right for sitting on, for looking at the passing of people, cars, and the passing of the day itself, or for just gazing off into space. On rainy days I would use them as banks from which to launch popsicle-stick ships into the streams that flowed along the gutters. Adventure-bound, these boats often disappeared between the iron bars of a drain, riding upon great waterfalling waves into the darkness, to continue their voyages beneath the earth.

After the run-off of spring rain, streaks of sandy dirt were often left behind in the gutters. Made up mostly of sand spread on the streets during the winter, these deposits sometimes took the wavy, rippled shape of the waters that had washed them into the gutter and that had flowed over and around them. As I would sit dreaming on a curbstone, it was pleasant to shuffle my sneakered feet in this sand, making little designs with it and feeling its softness against the hardness of the pavement. Putting my hands down by my sides, I could also feel the curbstone—the cool, smooth roughness, the solid reality of the world holding me. In the afternoon I would watch the stone's shadow move slowly from the curb's edge into the street along with my own. The sun-warmed sand would slowly cool in the shade and I would realize it was time to go home . . . Before going, I pick up a handful of sand and hold it in the fading sunlight, then let it run through my fingers back into the shadows.

>morning sunlight
under the Brooklyn Bridge
a curbstone shadow

*

The Sign

On a clear autumn day, alone by a small woods-encircled lake set in a high hollow between two peaks of the Catskill Mountains, I was looking for a sign, for some kind of tangible proof that the mystery I sometimes glimpse in the world of nature is not just something my mind puts there. Partly influenced by the little I knew of Zen and of American Indian vision quests, I had been praying, meditating, and fasting for several days—not for enlightenment or a vision, but for a sign I could reach out and touch, something "really" there.

There had been moments during my wanderings in the mountains when I thought I saw a flicker of the infinite in the shadows of a pine branch or sensed the fluttering of the eternal in the cool spruce-scented air of a sunlit ridge—but there had been nothing of which I could say: this is happening as a sign for me, because I am here and asking for it. I was still looking.

After exploring around the lake for some hours, clearing fallen leaves from the spring and exchanging looks with a curious frog, I was about to leave. Standing on a small grassy knoll at the edge, I gazed out over the quiet waters. Far beyond a rocky shelf of hemlocks at the other end (where a stream wound into the shadows and off a hidden ledge) the sun was nearing the mountain-ringed horizon. I raised my hand and said "Peace" to it all.

At the word, a small, bright light appeared over the lake, moving towards me through the air. It gradually took the shape of a large milkweed seed. Lit by the sun, yet seeming to shine from within, it rose from eye level and passed directly over my head, its white, tentacle-like hairs swaying slowly in the currents of air that carried it up over the trees and out of sight towards the top of Plattekill Mountain.

Thinking this was the answer to my prayers, I said a silent thanks to whatever had sent it and started along the trail to my campsite on the other side of the mountain. As I turned the first bend and lost sight of the lake, the cry of a large bird came from somewhere near the summit. Just once. The sun was going down now as I hurried through the forest, and it began to get dark as I came around to the mountain's shadow side.

A movement off to the right caught my eye. Two large grey wings rose a few feet above the forest floor, quickly glided deeper into the woods, and dropped down out of sight. Leaving the trail, I looked into the wooded ravine where the bird had vanished and even went down into it for about thirty or forty feet, but there was no sign of anything in the gathering darkness. Going back toward the trail, I started to step over a fallen log lying where the wings had first appeared. Something white was fluttering on it. A large milkweed seed glowed in the twilight, its feelers waving gently in the breeze. I didn't touch it, but it was still with me as I headed down the trail with the coming night.

    starlight in an empty milkweed pod

*

The Cricket

Midnight
September 9, 1982
129 East 10th Street (3rd floor)
Manhattan

Last night I caught a cricket in my living room. It was about this time of night, I was reading and I noticed a shadowy movement under the table. I thought at first it might be a large roach or even a waterbug—though I've seen neither in the year I've been here (except one tired-looking cockroach that looked as if it had gotten into my bathroom by mistake). But this moved differently and gave a hop when I came closer. Then hopped again. I cupped it in my hand and then contained it in an overturned glass while I prepared a little ventilated cardboard box for it about half the size of a brick with a glass cover. I put some small pieces of raw tomato and cucumber, a few kernels of cooked corn, some leaves and tassels from the corn, and some strawberry leaves in it and then transferred the cricket to it. There were some waterdrops on the food.

In the move the cricket lost one of its small wings or part of one. It curled up like a tiny flag. Unfurling it carefully with the tips of my fingers I spread out a tiny network of transparent lines and plates, similar to the glassy tapestry of a dragonfly's wing though it was smaller and more fan-shaped.

The cricket himself seemed not too upset by the loss or at least seemed not hampered in his movements about the box. After a few minutes search for a way out, he stopped by the corn kernels and began to munch at them.

I guess he came from the churchyard (St. Mark's West Yard) next door, but it is a bit of a mystery how he got up on the third floor. The first floor is three steps down from the street and there are some hedgelike shrubs in front of our building with a few flowers between those and the wall. But there is no grass or other ground cover in this area for a cricket to feel secure in. I suppose he could have come into this area from the churchyard, which has some large areas of leafy, evergreen ground cover, and then hopped down the three steps and into our entryway. But how did he get up two long flights of stairs? There is no elevator. Some crickets can fly but he gave no sign of being able to fly when he was hopping away from me. Did he hitchhike in on something?

He was a handsome creature, an earthy brown color, darkish and full-bodied, about the size of a full-grown hornet, the back legs almost as long as an inch if they had been straightened out—however they kept to the bent, ready-to-leap position. All the legs seemed well-barbed, and I wondered what kind of music he might make with them. But no, I remembered, crickets make their music with a part of their wings. Would the loss of that thin wing piece affect his singing? He stopped eating. His black eyes seemed to follow mine. I put his box about ten feet from my bed and went to sleep about an hour later.

I woke up about 3 AM to the pleasant sound of his chirping, a mellow musical note, each double chirp slowly paced with the next in a relaxing rhythm. I think he stopped after a few minutes. I woke again perhaps less than an hour later to hear him again for a few minutes before I slipped into sleep once more. He may have continued for a while afterwards for his singing was not disturbing, and I fell asleep while he was still calling gently into the darkness.

> falling asleep —
> the cricket's song follows me
> into my dreams

This evening I released him in a small overgrown park area near Washington Square Village, where to recreate the original flora of Manhattan, the city, or someone, has planted bushes, trees, and flowers and let them grow in wild profusion with lots of beautiful weeds and grasses. I was afraid to keep him in the box too long, for fear of weakening him or making him sick—I wasn't sure what to feed him either. I know the Japanese sometimes keep crickets in tiny cages to hear them sing (and also fireflies to see them light up). I think I read a poem about a cricket that died because the poet had forgotten to give it water.

The cricket did not leap out of the box when I opened it. I thought he might because he had jumped around in the kitchen last night when I had to recapture him. He had escaped as I was trying to move him into his box. But I guess leaping is for when he is trying to get away from something. He was now a little used to his box and he wanted to see, perhaps, what he was now going to get into. I held the open box inside the iron fence enclosing the "park preserve" so that it was close above the grasses and weeds. There was a little light from a streetlight nearby.

The cricket, looking black in the dusky light, crawled to the top edge of the box and seemed to look over and down at the vegetation below—and then just dropped down into it. I mentally wished him luck and brought the box back home in case there was another one about. As I left I could hear some crickets singing in the park area, and also one that seemed to be in the branch of a tree up on the lawn in front of one of the Washington Square Village apartment houses.

There was something lonely but reassuring about the way the darkness took the dark little creature in, and how he entered into it so gently and as though returning a part to the whole.

> the cricket's voice
> calls again and again from
> out of the darkness

*

The Squirrel

    Contributory streams of thought: a fragment from Roland Barthes, winding ways of words laid down by Herman Melville, observations by Rod Willmot upon the spiritual in haiku, images from Alan Pizzarelli of a blue bench on a merry-go-round and a rainbow of oil spreading from a piece of popcorn in a goldfish pond, my own whirligig duck flapping all summer in the breezes of Maine trying to get to the open sea or the grassy waterways of the salt marsh, the dreams of Thoreau and Emerson of coming to an opening where all is light forever, the pulsing throb of Whitman's universal heart beating among the stars like the roar of surf in the Milky Way, the swinging cascade of notes from Lester Young's saxophone as he turns a simple melody into a rippling masterpiece, the thought of no thought, in the silence of a Zen koan or in an immersion in the vibrations of Nichiren chanting, the travels of the mind into the emptiness of outer space or into the shadowy imagined corridor of a snail's shell: wherever the mind goes, it tries to find a place of its own, to make a place out of words, to make itself in words, to find itself in words, to lose itself in words.

    It wants something pure and visionary, perfect in form and harmony, and is surprised to find it in a squirrel sitting hunched on a limb of the horse-chestnut tree outside the kitchen window, protecting itself from a heavy thundershower by curling its tail up and over its back, nestling its nose in its two raised forepaws, the tip of the tail sticking out over its head like the peak of a cap, and a little eye opening now and again to look up at it.

>after the rain
>a few drops fall from the tree
>into the poet's notebook

*

The Singer

> Saturday, April 26, 1969
> New York City

Listened to a feathered Caruso today. A bird in a tree in Central Park (near the outdoor Shakespeare Theater). The bird was too high in the tree for me to identify it. Though I thought it looked like a robin, I couldn't believe it was a robin. Its song was so beautiful and varied: long, liquid trills; short, sweet burbles; soft, reedy piping; muted, string-like tones; round, full notes; a seemingly endless repertoire. Sometimes he would hit a phrase he liked, and would repeat it four or five times, but for the most part he would go directly from one invention to another. I listened to him for over an hour.

Though I kept him in sight all the time, even as he moved into three other trees and then back to the original one, he remained a mystery to me for almost an hour.

While he was in one of the other trees, another bird entered the branches a little below him. It looked to be of the same type. As soon as it entered the tree, the songster became quiet. Gradually the new bird came closer and closer to him. When they were about a yard apart, they began flirting about from branch to branch around each other. They then flew together to another tree. The singer then went to a blossoming cherry tree by himself and started singing again. Then back again to his favorite perch in the larger tree.

> the bird flies off
> from the now silent tree
> a few petals fall

One person passing by thought it might be a wood thrush, another thought it was an oriole, but one woman claimed it actually was a robin, for she had heard it a number of times during the day (in the same tree) and had got a good look at it. She said robins sometimes get so inspired in the spring, though the rest of the year their singing is mediocre. I enjoyed watching him as he sang, for the sun was getting low and the light in the budding branches around him was enchanting. The gentle breeze, cool, yet carrying the warmth of the spring sunshine, moved the light branch he was perched on and the sprays around him in the top of the tree softly. This calm motion, combined with the golden light and long shadows, and the enraptured music of the lone bird, completely enthralled me, and I thought of absolutely nothing for many magical moments.

Finally he dropped down from the tree and sailed directly toward where I was standing (I moved about the tree, sometimes standing, sometimes sitting, sometimes lying on the grass) and passed directly over my head, not more than three feet above it. I'm sure he was aware I'd been listening to him. He pulled up on the grass about 15 yards away and began hopping about for worms. He was a robin! His red breast was warmed by the setting sun. He cocked an eye in my direction and then went about getting his supper. When I left he was back in his tree singing away to the gathering shadows.

> the stars come out
> high in the budding tree
> the robin sings on

*

Yellow

I remember once when I was a little boy walking along a sidewalk in a quiet part of town. There was no one else around, no cars moving on the street and none, or few, parked along it. It was a bright, sunny morning in the summer. I came to a red fire hydrant and saw that the curbstone in front of it for about ten feet on either side had just been freshly painted a bright yellow. The paint glittered wetly. An open can was standing on the walk at one end of the painted stone. It was half-full of the brilliant paint, and its top edge glimmered with wet paint that had dripped in yellow petals partway down the outside. A brush still yellow with paint was lying on the turned-over cover next to the can. The painter was nowhere to be seen. The silence was immense.

Somehow the sunshine of that day shone with and in that yellow paint with such a primal light that it still shines down through the years in my mind: the wet band of golden stone blazing coolly in the middle of a day of magic sunshine—and the yellow can blooming at one end of it like a great golden flower.

> a breeze off the lake
> the stepped-on dandelion
> pushes itself back up

*

Snowstorm

After the long snowfall has silenced the East Village, the streetlights hold the snowy streets in a stillness of softly glowing curves and mounds of snow. Out of everyday objects the snow has created new shapes and landscapes. Garbage cans are white pillars of rounded snow. The cars parked along East Tenth Street have become sloping hills all joined together. The street itself is a still river of white, the snow now too deep for traffic. The building fronts, from steps to eaves, and their iron fences and gates have all been transformed into ornate filigrees of snow. The snow decorates the bare branches of the sidewalk trees so that gingkoes, oaks, and flowering pears are now all snow trees. There is no wind. Only a single person is out walking and now he too is still. The street glows silently in the lamplight.

> city street
> the darkness inside
> the snow-covered cars

*

Puddles

haru no hi ya mizu sae areba kure nokori
wherever there is water, the spring day lingers
into evening
— Kobayashi Issa

the shallowest still water is unfathomable

—Henry David Thoreau

Puddles or pools—in the woods, on the seashore, or on city streets or sidewalks—have long fascinated and intrigued me, stirred strange longings, inexplicable feelings, a quietly joyful conviction that I'm looking into the mystery of existence.

It can happen at any season, even in New York City: on hot, sunny days in summer, when someone has hosed down a sidewalk, leaving a small pool glittering darkly in the gutter, a cool open window on eternity, its calm acceptance contrasting with the harsh glare bouncing from the chrome of parked cars; or on a dark, drizzling day in autumn when puddles are everywhere, in construction-site excavations and on pavements in front of Broadway theaters, scattered through the park and on the roofs of brownstones, glowing with a shallow crystal clarity on window ledges, or unreeling a dark reflective film on the flat metal railings of fire escapes; or in winter or spring when melting snow leaves water under bushes or hedges or among the broken bricks and withered grasses of a vacant lot, or under a small yew in a wooden tub in front of a hotel on Lexington Avenue.

However they are formed—from rain, snow, or a broken fireplug—they are always full of magic; under cloudy or clearing skies, or even at night beneath the stars. If sunlit, the pools are full of light and air, or folding a shadow of a shadow into the earth. Under overcast skies they have a cold light of their own as if they have absorbed all the available light out of the atmosphere. At night their darkness seems to drop deep into a galaxy of other worlds spinning with a faint frosting of light that moves dimly in and out of sight far below the surface.

These pools—whether in the form of a lake or a drop of rain on a leaf or a crooked puddle in the dent of a garbage can lid—must be clear. Muddy puddles do not hold my interest; the doors, or the curtains, are closed. But whatever its size or shape, a body of clear water will hold me entranced, and I must stop for at least a few moments whenever I meet one—or for as long as it holds me, lifts me, and then lets me go.

1. The Side of the Road

It is getting towards evening after a drizzly day of hiking. Just ahead of me, by the side of the road, there is a puddle of clear water. Placed between the woods and the pavement, in the sand and dirt of the road's shoulder, it presents an aspect of loneliness and solitude that complements and intensifies my own, and a sad happiness grows in me as I recognize my mood in the landscape around me. Under the overcast sky, the water's crystal emptiness fills with a muted light, a light that comes from something alone and eternal. The puddle itself is temporary—like me—and will soon be gone. I stop on the deserted highway as dusk comes down and look long into the clear water. And I find a purity and peace that will sustain me for many miles to come.

> dawn
> a floating maple leaf
> slowly turns

*

2. The Window-Washer's Pail

On a side street in Manhattan, a window-washer is getting ready to clean the windows of a small storefront. It is a bright spring morning, with a cool blue sky and a few white clouds scudding here and there. A new looking galvanized-metal pail stands glittering on the sidewalk. Inside, the metal glows under clear water. Sunlight is just leaning into the pail, throwing a shadow from a floating sponge down into the water and onto the sides of the pail. There are also small shadows on the irregular surface of the sponge. A breeze gently sails it across the waters of the pail.

> between splashes
> water in the pothole
> reflects a cloud

*

3. Passing

A clear puddle on the sidewalk covers a small iron valve-cover with the raised letters WATER across it. Seeing the word through and in that which it means or stands for seems to hold a special meaning for me. As I gaze into the pool, and as passersby, I suppose, pass by, glimmerings of the power of words and the power of natural phenomena intermingle in my mind. The word becoming the thing, the thing in the word—here is the word in the thing—the magic of poetry and nature seem somehow combining to tell me something about reality and the human mind. Suddenly I realize that the water is disappearing! Not that I can see it doing so, but invisible molecules are continually taking off from this small pool, like seeds from a thistle, into the atmosphere. In several hours there will be nothing but a dusty sidewalk and an uncovered word. The pool will be gone, perhaps floating in a cloud far out over the ocean or above a mountain away off in the Catskills.

> in the mountains
> a roadhouse sign goes out
> clouds blow off the stars

*

4. A Tidepool

A grey autumn day. A chill wind blows along the deserted beach in Wells, Maine. It is low tide, and a huge boulder leans about four feet high out of the damp sand. In a curved depression around its base, carved in the sand by the swirling tide, the ocean has left a cold tidepool that the wind ripples all afternoon. The clear grey water under the grey overcast sky seems shaken with all the loneliness of existence. The most distant corners of the universe are somehow here in this small, moving, yet unmoving, pool that will—when the tide returns—again be one with the ocean.

> at the closed drive-in — rain in a bottlecap

*

5. On the Mountain

The fringes of the timberline—grasses and small spruces and firs—cling to the rocky cliffs at the top of Mount Kinsman in New Hampshire's White Mountains. There is a spring in a hollow just below the summit ledge, in among some of the taller of the dwarfed trees. I look through the water as if through a space of heightened nothingness and see a few rocks and a little drift of sand loom from the bottom with such clarity they seem to belong to another dimension. The pool is a nothing that contains everything: the stars and moon appear there at night, the sky and clouds wander through it during the day—and each morning the sun sends a light dimly down through the trees and into its transparent depths. Now I, too, try to plumb these few inches of nothing, and find them opening into a view of endless space where the water and I are one and the same. I turn and look off into the distance to see mountain peaks after mountain peaks going in long ranks all about me, but not even the most distant, somewhere in far New York, can take my mind and eye so far as this little pool under the spruce trees.

> a Monarch flutters
> to the top of a trailmarker
> pointing south

*

Credits

The haibun below first appeared in the following publications:

"The Sign" in *Modern Haiku*, vol. xix, no. 3, Autumn 1988.

"Curbstones" in *Modern Haiku*, vol. xxiii, no. 2, Summer 1992.

"The Cricket" in *Woodnotes*, no. 21, Summer 1994.

"The Squirrel" in *Tundra,* December 2001.

"Hitchhiking" and "Snowstorm" both appeared in *Summer Dreams: American Haibun & Haiga*, by Jim Kacian, Red Moon Press, © 2002.

"Yellow" in *Journeys,* no. 1, Spring 2002.

"The Katydid" in *bottle rockets*, vol. 14, no. 2 (#28), 2013.

"The Last Streetlight" in *bottle rockets*, no. 29, 2013.

Printed in Great Britain
by Amazon